Vermont Ecoregions

- Eastern Great Lakes Lowlands
- Northeastern Highlands

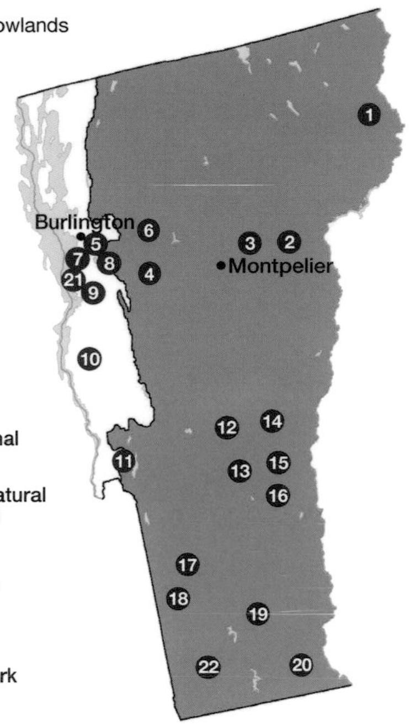

1. Maidstone State Park
2. Groton State Forest
3. Greatwood Gardens/ Goddard College
4. Camel's Hump State Park
5. Vermont Community Botanic Gardens
6. Underhill State Park
7. Shelburne Farms National Historic Landmark
8. H. Lawrence Achilles Natural Area at Shelburne Pond
9. Mt. Philo State Park
10. Wilmarth Woods/Snake Mountain
11. Bomoseen State Park
12. Gifford Woods State Park
13. Coolidge State Park
14. Marsh-Billings-Rockefeller National Historical Park
15. Eshqua Bog Natural Area
16. Ascutney State Park
17. Emerald Lake State Park
18. Boswell Botany Trail at Southern Vermont Arts Center
19. Townshend State Park/Bald Mountain
20. Black Mountain Natural Area
21. Vermont Wildflower Farm
22. Southern Vermont Natural History Museum

Measurements denote the height of plants unless otherwise indicated. Illustrations are not to scale.

N.B. – Many edible wild plants have poisonous mimics. Never eat a wild plant or fruit unless you are absolutely sure it is safe to do so. The publisher makes no representation or warranties with respect to the accuracy, completeness, correctness or usefulness of this information and specifically disclaims any implied warranties of fitness for a particular purpose. The advice, strategies and/or techniques contained herein may not be suitable for all individuals. The publisher shall not be responsible for any physical harm (up to and including death), loss of profit or other commercial damage. The publisher assumes no liability brought or instituted by individuals or organizations arising out of or relating in any way to the application and/or use of the information, advice and strategies contained herein.

Made in the USA

Waterford Press publishes reference guides to nature observation, outdoor recreation and survival skills. Product information is featured on the website: **www.waterfordpress.com**

Text & illustrations © 2009, 2021 Waterford Press Inc. All rights reserved.
Photos © Shutterstock. Ecoregion map © The National Atlas of the United States.

To order or for information on custom published products please call 800-434-2555 or email orderdesk@waterfordpress.com.
For permissions or to share comments email editor@waterfordpress.com.

ISBN 978-1-58355-518-7 $7.95 U.S.
50795
9 781583 555187
UPC 8 84682 01132 1
10 9 8 7 6 5 4 3 2 1
217134

VERMONT TREES & WILDFLOWERS – A Folding Pocket Guide to Familiar Plants

Kavanagh/Leung

A POCKET NATURALIST® GUIDE

VERMONT
TREES & WILDFLOWERS

A Folding Pocket Guide to Familiar Plants

T0124001

TREES & SHRUBS

Balsam Fir
Abies balsamea To 60 ft. (18 m)
Flattened needles grow around branchlets in 2 rows. Purplish cones grow upright.

Tamarack
Larix laricina To 80 ft. (24 m)
Needles grow in tufts. Stalkless cones grow upright. One of the only conifers to shed its needles in winter.

Black Spruce
Picea mariana To 75 ft. (23 m)
Small to medium-sized tree has 4-sided needles that are about .5 in. (1.3 cm) long.

Red Spruce
Picea rubens To 80 ft. (24 m)
Note conical crown of silhouette. 4-sided flattened needles have sharp points and grow singly along branchlets.

Red Pine
Pinus resinosa To 80 ft. (24 m)
Flexible needles are up to 6 in. (15 cm) long and grow in bundles of two. Common in sandy soils.

Pitch Pine
Pinus rigida To 60 ft. (18 m)
Long needles grow in bundles of 3. Cone scales have stiff, curved spines. Bark is rich with resin (pitch).

Eastern White Pine
Pinus strobus To 100 ft. (30 m)
Needles grow in bundles of 5. Cone is up to 8 in. (20 cm) long.

Eastern Hemlock
Tsuga canadensis To 70 ft. (21 m)
Flat needles grow from 2 sides of twigs, parallel to the ground. Tip of tree usually droops.

Eastern Redcedar
Juniperus virginiana To 60 ft. (18 m)
4-sided branchlets are covered with overlapping, scale-like leaves. Fruit is a blue berry.

Northern White-cedar
Thuja occidentalis To 70 ft. (21 m)
Drooping branchlets are covered with scale-like leaves. Wood is aromatic.

Common Juniper
Juniperus communis To 4 ft. (1.2 m)
Needle-like leaves grow in whorls of 3 around twigs. Berry-like, blue-black cones have 1–3 seeds.

Balsam Poplar
Populus balsamifera
To 80 ft. (24 m)
Drooping flower clusters are succeeded by oval capsules containing cottony seeds.

TREES & SHRUBS

Bigtooth Aspen
Populus grandidentata To 60 ft. (18 m)
Leaves have large, blunt teeth along the edges. Brownish flowers bloom in a long cluster and are succeeded by small capsules.

Trembling Aspen
Populus tremuloides To 70 ft. (21 m)
Long-stemmed leaves rustle in the slightest breeze. The most widely distributed tree in North America.

Black Willow
Salix nigra To 100 ft. (30 m)
Tree or shrub, often leaning. Slender leaves are shiny green on the upper surface. Flowers bloom in long, fuzzy clusters.

Butternut
Juglans cinerea To 70 ft. (21 m)
Leaves have 11–17 leaflets. Oval fruits are 4-ribbed.

White Willow
Salix alba To 80 ft. (24 m)
Introduced ornamental has slender leaves. Flowers bloom in long catkins and are succeeded by seed capsules.

Paper Birch
Betula papyrifera To 70 ft. (21 m)
Whitish bark peels off trunk in thin sheets. Bark was used by Native Americans to make bowls and canoes.

Yellow Birch
Betula alleghaniensis
To 100 ft. (30 m)
Bark is red to yellowish and peels off in strips. Cone-like oval fruit grows erect on branchlets.

Gray Birch
Betula populifolia To 30 ft. (9 m)
Small tree has a spindly trunk and an open irregular crown. A pioneer species that establishes itself quickly in poor soils.

Eastern Hophornbeam
Ostrya virginiana To 50 ft. (15 m)
Trunk has sinewy, muscle-like bark. Hop-like fruits are hanging, cone-like clusters.

American Beech
Fagus grandifolia To 80 ft. (24 m)
Flowers bloom in rounded clusters in spring and are succeeded by 3-sided nuts.

Northern Red Oak
Quercus rubra To 90 ft. (27 m)
Large tree has a rounded crown. Leaves have 7–11 spiny lobes.

Alder
Alnus spp. To 40 ft. (12 m)
Shrub or tree often forms dense thickets. Flowers bloom in long clusters and are succeeded by distinctive, cone-like woody fruits.

TREES & SHRUBS

American Elm
Ulmus americana To 100 ft. (30 m)
Note vase-shaped profile. Leaves are toothed. Fruits have a papery collar and are notched at the tip.

Common Serviceberry
Amelanchier arborea To 40 ft. (12 m)
White, star-shaped flowers bloom early in spring. Red to purple-black berries ripen in mid-summer.

Hawthorn
Crataegus spp. To 40 ft. (12 m)
Tree has rounded crown of spiny branches. Apple-like fruits appear in summer.

Black Cherry
Prunus serotina To 80 ft. (24 m)
Aromatic bark and leaves smell cherry-like. Dark berries have an oval stone inside.

Boxelder
Acer negundo To 60 ft. (18 m)
Leaves have 3–7 leaflets. Seeds are encased in paired papery keys.

Striped Maple
Acer pensylvanicum To 30 ft. (9 m)
Shrub or small tree is distinguished by its white-striped, bright green bark.

Red Maple
Acer rubrum To 90 ft. (27 m)
Leaves have 3–5 lobes and turn scarlet in autumn. Flowers are succeeded by red, winged seed pairs.

Sugar Maple
Acer saccharum To 100 ft. (30 m)
Leaves have five coarsely-toothed lobes. Fruit is a winged seed pair. Tree sap is the source of maple syrup.
Vermont's state tree.

American Basswood
Tilia americana To 100 ft. (30 m)
Leaves are heart-shaped. Flowers and nutlets hang from narrow leafy bracts.

Black Ash
Fraxinus nigra To 50 ft. (15 m)
Leaves have 7–11 leaflets. Fruit is a winged seed.

Witch Hazel
Hamamelis virginiana To 30 ft. (9 m)
Shrub or small tree. Leaves turn yellow in autumn. Fruits are woody capsules with 4 sharp points.

American Mountain-ash
Sorbus americana To 30 ft. (9 m)
Leaves have 13–17 leaflets. Red fruits occur in dense clusters.

TREES & SHRUBS

Rosebay Rhododendron
Rhododendron maximum To 40 ft. (12 m)
Evergreen leaves are thick and leathery. White to pink flowers bloom in dense clusters. Found in northern Vermont.

Azalea
Rhododendron roseum To 10 ft. (3 m)
Leaves are woolly beneath. Flowers are white or pink. Found in the south.

Pin Cherry
Prunus pensylvanica To 30 ft. (9 m)
Lance-shaped leaves have curled margins. Small clusters of whitish flowers are succeeded by bright red berries.

Common Chokecherry
Prunus virginiana To 20 ft. (6 m)
Cylindrical clusters of spring flowers are succeeded by dark, red-purple berries.

Blackberry
Rubus allegheniensis
To 10 ft. (3 m)
Leaves usually have 3 leaflets. White flowers are succeeded by red berries that blacken when ripe.

Smooth Sumac
Rhus glabra
To 20 ft. (6 m)
Clusters of white flowers are succeeded by "hairy" red fruits. Bark is gray and smooth.

Pussy Willow
Salix discolor
To 20 ft. (6 m)
Distinctive fuzzy catkins appear in spring before the leaves.

Wild Red Raspberry
Rubus idaeus
To 6 ft. (1.8 m)
Leaves have 3–5 leaflets. Fruits appear in summer.

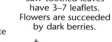

Red-Osier Dogwood
Cornus sericea
To 10 ft. (3 m)
White flowers are succeeded by waxy white berries. Bark is reddish.

Elderberry
Sambucus spp.
To 16 ft. (4.8 m)
Saw-toothed leaves have 3–7 leaflets. Flowers are succeeded by dark berries.

Possumhaw
Viburnum nudum
To 16 ft. (4.8 m)
Tiny flowers are succeeded by berries that may be pink or blue-black.

Blueberry
Vaccinium spp.
To 2 ft. (60 cm)
Low, mat-forming shrub.

Winterberry Holly
Ilex verticillata
To 25 ft. (7.6 m)
Common bog plant.

WHITE & GREENISH FLOWERS

Yarrow
Achillea millefolium
To 3 ft. (90 cm)
Leaves are fern-like.
Each tiny flower
has 4–6 rays.

Showy Lady's Slipper
Cypripedium reginae
To 3 ft. (90 cm)

Pussytoes
Antennaria spp.
To 16 in. (40 cm)
Woolly stalks support
fluffy flowerheads.

Labrador Tea
Rhododendron groenlandicum
To 30 in. (75 cm)
Leaves have rolled
edges and are
rust-colored
and hairy below.

Pearly Everlasting
Anaphalis margaritacea
To 3 ft. (90 cm)
Creamy flowers bloom
in large terminal clusters.

Lamb's Quarters
Chenopodium album
To 6 ft. (1.8 m)
Small cauliflower-like
white flowers bloom
in dense clusters.
Also called "pigweed."

Jack-in-the-Pulpit
Arisaema triphyllum
To 3 ft. (90 cm)
Club-like stem is
surrounded by a curving,
green to purplish hood.

Bunchberry
Cornus canadensis
To 8 in. (20 cm)
Leaves grow in whorls of
4–6. Small white flowers are
succeeded by
bright red berries.

Queen Anne's Lace
Daucus carota
To 4 ft. (1.2 m)
Flower clusters become
cup-shaped as they age.

Bloodroot
Sanguinaria canadensis
To 10 in. (25 cm)
Blooms in early spring.

Wild Strawberry
Fragaria spp.
Stems to 8 in. (20 cm)
Creeping plant has
5-petalled flowers
that are succeeded
by the familiar fruit.

Wood Anemone
Anemone quinquefolia
To 8 in. (20 cm)
Found in moist
meadows and woods.

Cow Parsnip
Heracleum lanatum
To 9 ft. (2.7 m)
Large leaves are
deeply lobed. Creamy
white flowers bloom in
dense, flattened clusters.

WHITE & GREENISH FLOWERS

Oxeye Daisy
Leucanthemum vulgare
To 3 ft. (90 cm)
Showy flowers bloom
along roadsides
in summer.

Dutchman's Breeches
Dicentra cucullaria
To 12 in. (30 cm)
Spurred flowers
resemble trousers.

Nodding Ladies' Tresses
Spiranthes cernua
To 2 ft. (60 cm)
Flowers bloom
in spiral rows on
flower stalk.

Bladder Campion
Silene vulgaris
To 30 in. (75 cm)
Flowers bloom at
tip of melon-like
swelling.

Large-flowered Trillium
Trillium grandiflorum
To 18 in. (45 cm)
3 white petals turn
pinkish with age.

Foam Flower
Tiarella cordifolia
To 12 in. (30 cm)

Painted Trillium
Trillium undulatum

YELLOW & ORANGE FLOWERS

Marsh Marigold
Caltha palustris
To 2 ft. (60 cm)
Aquatic plant has large,
heart-shaped leaves and
bright yellow flowers.

Trout Lily
Erythronium americanum
To 10 in. (25 cm)
Common in meadows
and rich woodlands.

Yellow Lady's Slipper
Cypripedium calceolus
To 28 in. (70 cm)

Orange Hawkweed
Hieracium aurantiacum
To 2 ft. (60 cm)
Hairy plant has leaves
clustered at its base.

Large-flowered Bellwort
Uvularia grandiflora
To 20 in. (50 cm)

Canada Lily
Lilium canadense
To 5 ft. (1.5 m)

Sneezeweed
Helenium spp.
To 20 in. (50 cm)
Yellow flowers have a
dome-like central disk.

YELLOW & ORANGE FLOWERS

Downy Yellow Violet
Viola pubescens
To 16 in.
(35 cm)

Yellow Sweet Clover
Melilotus officinalis
To 5 ft. (1.5 m)
Yellow pea-like
flowers bloom
on densely
packed spikes.

Butter-and-Eggs
Linaria vulgaris
To 3 ft. (90 cm)
Spurred flowers
have a patch of
orange in the
throat.

Fringed Loosestrife
Lysimachia ciliata
To 4 ft. (1.2 m)
Named for its
fringed petals.

Yellow Wood Sorrel
Oxalis stricta
To 15 in. (38 cm)
Leaves are clover-like.
Fruits look like
candlesticks.

Evening Primrose
Oenothera spp.
To 5 ft. (1.5 m)
Lemon-scented,
4-petalled flowers
bloom in the evening.

Common Mullein
Verbascum thapsus
To 7 ft. (2.1 m)
Common roadside weed.

Yellow Pond Lily
Nuphar lutea
Flower to 2.5 in.
(6 cm) wide.
Floating aquatic plant.

Black-eyed Susan
Rudbeckia hirta
To 3 ft. (90 cm)
Flower has a dark,
conical central disk.

Buttercup
Ranunculus spp.
To 3 ft. (90 cm)
Flower petals are
waxy to the touch.

Large-flowered Bellwort

Golden Alexanders
Zizia aurea
To 3 ft. (90 cm)
Small flowers bloom
in flat-topped clusters.

Coltsfoot
Tussilago farfara
To 18 in. (45 cm)
Low-growing herb
has asparagus-like
stems. Basal leaves
are heart-shaped.

PINK & RED FLOWERS

Hog Peanut
Amphicarpaea bracteata
Vine to 4 ft. (1.2 m)

Swamp Milkweed
Asclepias incarnata
To 4 ft. (1.2 m)
Plant has milky sap.

Wild Ginger
Asarum canadense
To 12 in. (30 cm)
Flowers arise at base
of 2 leaves.

Red Columbine
Aquilegia canadensis
To 2 ft. (60 cm)

Water Smartweed
Polygonum amphibium
Stems to 4 ft. (1.2 m) long.
Aquatic plant blooms in
nearshore waters.

Hedge Bindweed
Convolvulus sepium
Vine to 10 ft. (3 m)

Pink Lady's Slipper
Cypripedium acaule
To 14 in. (35 cm)

Deptford Pink
Dianthus armeria
To 2 ft. (60 cm)
Slender stems
support loose
clusters of star-like
pink flowers.

Cardinal Flower
Lobelia cardinalis
To 4 ft. (1.2 m)

Showy Tick Trefoil
Desmodium canadense
To 6 ft. (1.8 m)

Fireweed
Chamerion angustifolium
To 10 ft. (3 m)
Common in open
woodlands and
waste areas.

Spring Beauty
Claytonia virginica
To 12 in. (30 cm)

Wild Mint
Mentha arvensis
To 31 in. (78 cm)
Lavender to white
flowers grow in
clusters at leaf bases.

Red Clover
Trifolium pratense
To 2 ft. (60 cm)
Leaves have
3 leaflets.
Vermont's
state flower.

PINK & RED FLOWERS

Joe-Pye Weed
Eutrochium maculatum
To 7 ft. (2.1 m)
Flowers are pink to
purple. Leaves grow in
whorls of 3–5.

Phlox
Phlox spp. To 20 in. (50 cm)
Five-petalled,
yellow-centered flowers may
be white, yellow, pink, red
or lavender. Grows in
sprawling clusters.

Sheep Laurel
Kalmia angustifolia
To 3 ft. (90 cm)

Canada Thistle
Cirsium arvense
To 5 ft. (1.5 m)

Bouncing Bet
Saponaria officinalis
To 3 ft. (90 cm)
Flowers are pinkish
to white.

Red Trillium
Trillium erectum
To 16 in. (40 cm)
Flowers smell of
rotting flesh.

BLUE & PURPLE FLOWERS

Harebell
Campanula rotundifolia
To 40 in. (1 m)

Chicory
Cichorium intybus
To 10 ft. (3 m)
Wheel-shaped
flowers are varying
shades of blue.

Blueweed
Echium vulgare
To 30 in. (75 cm)
Blue flowers have
long, red stamens.
Also called viper's
bugloss. Invasive.

New England Aster
Aster novae-angliae
To 7 ft. (2.1 m)

Bluets
Houstonia caerulea
To 6 in. (15 cm)
Yellow-centered flowers
grow in large colonies.

Blue Flag
Iris versicolor
To 3 ft. (90 cm)

Wild Geranium
Geranium spp.
To 2 ft. (60 cm)

BLUE & PURPLE FLOWERS

Spiked Lobelia
Lobelia spicata
To 4 ft. (1.2 m)

Allegheny Monkeyflower
Mimulus ringens
To 3 ft. (90 cm)
Bluish, yellow-centered
flowers have a
puffy lower lip.

Wild Bergamot
Monarda fistulosa
To 4 ft. (1.2 m)

Purple Loosestrife
Lythrum salicaria
To 7 ft. (2.1 m)
Invasive weed is
very common in
marshes and ponds.

Forget-me-not
Myosotis scorpioides
To 2 ft. (60 cm)
Small sky-blue flowers
have yellow centers.

Blue-eyed Grass
Sisyrinchium spp.
To 20 in. (50 cm)

Blue Vervain
Verbena hastata
To 6 ft. (1.8 m)
Has a slender spike
of bluish flowers.

Northern Pitcher Plant
Sarracenia purpurea
To 2 ft. (60 cm)
Carnivorous plant has
cup-shaped leaves
that trap insects.

Cow Vetch
Vicia cracca
Stems to 7 ft. (2.1 m) long.
Sprawling plant has
pea-shaped flowers.

Bittersweet Nightshade
Solanum dulcamara
Vine to 10 ft. (3 m) long.
Purplish flowers have
a yellow "beak."

Common Blue Violet
Viola sororia
To 8 in. (20 cm)

Pickerelweed
Pontederia cordata
To 4 ft. (1.2 m)
Aquatic plant has dense
spike of blue flowers.

Fringed Gentian
Gentianopsis crinita
To 3 ft. (90 cm)

Wild Blue Phlox
Phlox divaricata
To 20 in. (50 cm)

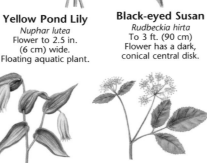

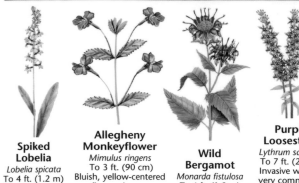

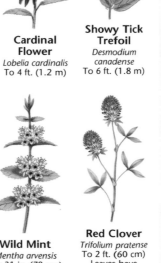

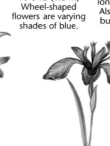
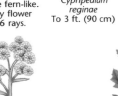